## What Happens in Spring?
# Birds in Spring
by Jenny Fretland VanVoorst

Bullfrog Books

# Ideas for Parents and Teachers

Bullfrog Books let children practice reading informational text at the earliest reading levels. Repetition, familiar words, and photo labels support early readers.

## Before Reading

- Discuss the cover photo. What does it tell them?
- Look at the picture glossary together. Read and discuss the words.

## Read the Book

- "Walk" through the book and look at the photos. Let the child ask questions. Point out the photo labels.
- Read the book to the child, or have him or her read independently.

## After Reading

- Prompt the child to think more. Ask: Have you ever seen a nest with eggs in it? Did you see it after the eggs had hatched?

Bullfrog Books are published by Jump!
5357 Penn Avenue South
Minneapolis, MN 55419
www.jumplibrary.com

Library of Congress Cataloging-in-Publication Data

Fretland VanVoorst, Jenny, 1972– author.
  Birds in spring / by Jenny Fretland VanVoorst.
     pages cm. — (What happens in spring?)
  "Bullfrog Books are published by Jump!"
  Audience: Ages 5–8.
  Audience: K to grade 3.
  Includes bibliographical references and index.
  ISBN 978-1-62031-235-3 (hardcover: alk. paper) —
  ISBN 978-1-62496-322-3 (ebook)
  1.  Birds—Behavior—Juvenile literature.
  2.  Spring—Juvenile literature.  I. Title.
  QL698.3.F68 2015
  598.156—dc23

                                        2014044017

Series Designer: Ellen Huber
Book Designer: Michelle Sonnek
Photo Researcher: Michelle Sonnek

Photo Credits: All photos by Shutterstock except: age fotostock, 14–15; Corbis, 1; Dreamstime, 12–13; Glow Images, 4; SuperStock, 13; Thinkstock, 24; Whitney Hartshorne/Flickr, 11.

Printed in the United States of America at Corporate Graphics in North Mankato, Minnesota.

# Table of Contents

# Busy Birds

It is spring.

The air warms.

Trees grow leaves.
Flowers bloom.

Birds return from
the South.

It is time to mate.

The male sings.

The female hears him.

She likes his song.

They mate.

The birds build a nest.

They use mud and grass.

10

The female lays eggs.

11

She sits on the eggs.

She keeps them warm.

In 14 days they hatch.

The baby birds
want food.

They open their
beaks and cry.

Mom brings them a bug.
She chews it first.

16

Then she feeds them.
Yum!

The babies have grown.
Look at their feathers!

They spread their wings.
It is time to fly!

# Parts of a Bird

**feathers**
Light, fluffy parts that cover a bird's body.

**wings**
One of the feather-covered limbs a bird flaps in order to fly.

**beak**
The hard, horny part of a bird's mouth.

**claw**
A hard, curved, sharp nail on a bird's foot.

# Picture Glossary

**hatch**
To break out
of an egg.

**South**
The warm part
of the world
where some
birds spend
the winter.

**mate**
To join together
to make young.

**spread**
To stretch out.

# Index

# To Learn More

Learning more is as easy as 1, 2, 3.

1) Go to www.factsurfer.com

2) Enter "birdsinspring" into the search box.

3) Click the "Surf" button to see a list of websites.

With factsurfer.com, finding more information is just a click away.